GW00514794

ONE HUNDRED
FAVOURITE
COMIC POEMS

First published in hardback in the United Kingdom in 2003 by
Frith Book Company Ltd

Paperback edition 2004
ISBN 1-85937-932-X

British Library Cataloguing in Publication Data
One Hundred Favourite Comic Poems
ISBN 1-85937-932-X

Frith Book Company Ltd
Frith's Barn, Teffont,
Salisbury, Wiltshire SP3 5QP
Tel: +44 (0) 1722 716 376
Email: info@francisfrith.co.uk
www.francisfrith.co.uk

Printed and bound in Spain

CONTENTS

Three Clerihews about Famous Men

SIR Christopher Wren
Said, 'I am going to dine with some men.
If anybody calls
Say I am designing St Paul's.'

GEORGE the Third
Ought never to have occurred.
One can only wonder
At so grotesque a blunder.

SIR Humphry Davy
Abominated gravy.
He lived in the odium
Of having discovered Sodium.

E C BENTLEY (1875-1956)

Limerick about Travel

THERE was a young girl, a sweet lamb,
Who smiled as she entered a tram.
      After she had embarked,
      The conductor remarked:
'Your fare!' And she said, 'Yes, I am.'

ANON

Two More Limericks about Travel

DETERMINISM

THERE was a young man who said, 'Damn!'
It appears to me now that I am
    Just a being that moves
    In predestinate grooves,
Not a taxi or bus, but a tram.

RELATIVITY

THERE was a young lady named Bright,
Who travelled much faster than light,
    She started one day
    In the relative way,
And returned on the previous night.

ANON

On the Ning Nang Nong

ON THE Ning Nang Nong
Where the Cows go Bong!
And the Monkeys all say Boo!
There's a Nong Nang Ning
Where the trees go Ping!
And the tea pots Jibber Jabber Joo.
On the Nong Ning Nang
All the mice go Clang!
And you just can't catch 'em when they do!
So it's Ning Nang Nong!
Cows go Bong!
Nong Nang Ning!
Trees go Ping!
Nong Ning Nang!
The mice go Clang!
What a noisy place to belong,
Is the Ning Nang Ning Nang Nong!!

SPIKE MILLIGAN (1918-2002)

Fool's Song

WHEN swallows lay their eggs in snow,
    And geese in wheat-ears build their nests;
When roasted crabs a-hunting go,
    And cats can laugh at gossips' jests;
When law and conscience are akin,
    And pigs are learnt by note to squeak;
Your worship then shall stroke your chin,
    And teach an owl to whistle Greek.

Till when let your wisdom be dumb;
    For say, man of Gotham,
      What is this world?
      A tetotum,
    By the finger of Folly twirled;
With a hey-go-up, and about we come;
While the sun a good post-horse is found,
So merrily we'll run round.

When frost, and snow, and hail, and rain,
    Are guided by the Almanack;
When Lapland wizards can explain
    How many stars will fill a sack;
When courtiers hate to be preferred,
    And pearls are made of whitings' eyes;
Instructed by your worship's beard,
    The world shall merry be and wise.

THOMAS HOLCROFT (1745-1809)

Turtle Soup

BEAUTIFUL Soup, so rich and green,
    Waiting in a hot tureen!
Who for such dainties would not stoop?
Soup of the evening, beautiful Soup!
Soup of the evening, beautiful Soup!
    Beau—ootiful Soo—oop!
    Beau—ootiful Soo—oop!
Soo—oop of the e—e—evening,
    Beautiful, beautiful Soup!

Beautiful Soup! Who cares for fish,
    Game or any other dish?
Who would not give all else for two p-
ennyworth only of beautiful Soup?
Pennyworth only of beautiful Soup?
    Beau—ootiful Soo—oop!
    Beau—ootiful Soo—oop!
Soo—oop of the e—e—evening,
    Beautiful, beauti—FUL SOUP!

LEWIS CARROLL (1832-1898)

The Mad Gardener's Song

HE THOUGHT he saw an Elephant,
    That practised on a fife:
He looked again, and found it was
    A letter from his wife.
'At length I realize,' he said,
    'The bitterness of Life!'

He thought he saw a Buffalo
    Upon the chimney-piece:
He looked again, and found it was
    His Sister's Husband's Niece.
'Unless you leave this house,' he said,
    'I'll send for the Police!'…

He thought he saw an Argument
    That proved he was the Pope:
He looked again, and found it was
    A Bar of Mottled Soap.
'A fact so dread,' he faintly said,
    'Extinguishes all hope!'

LEWIS CARROLL (1832-1898)

The Terns

SAID the mother Tern
      to her baby Tern
Would you like a brother?
Said baby Tern
      to mother Tern
Yes
One good Tern deserves another.

SPIKE MILLIGAN (1918-2002)

The Common Cormorant

THE common cormorant or shag
Lays eggs inside a paper bag.
The reason you will see, no doubt,
It is to keep the lightning out.
But what these unobservant birds
Have never noticed is that herds
Of wandering bears may come with buns
And steal the bags to hold the crumbs.

ANON

Limerick about the Pelican

A WONDERFUL bird is the pelican,
His mouth can hold more than his belican.
    He can take in his beak
    Enough food for a week—
I'm damned if I know how the helican.

ANON

I Saw a Peacock

I SAW a peacock with a fiery tail
I saw a blazing comet drop down hail
I saw a cloud with ivy circled round
I saw a sturdy oak creep on the ground
I saw a pismire swallow up a whale
I saw a raging sea brim full of ale
I saw a Venice glass sixteen foot deep
I saw a well full of men's tears that weep
I saw their eyes all in a flame of fire
I saw a house as big as the moon and higher
I saw the sun even in the midst of night
I saw the man that saw this wondrous sight.

ANON

If All the World were Paper

IF ALL the world were paper,
And all the sea were ink,
And all the trees were bread and cheese,
What should we do for drink?

If all the world were sand-o
Oh, then what should we lack-o;
If as they say there were no clay,
How should we take tobacco?

If all our vessels ran-a,
If none but had a crack-a,
If Spanish apes ate all the grapes,
What should we do for sack-a?

If friars had no bald pates,
Nor nuns had no dark cloisters,
If all the seas were beans and peas,
What should we do for oysters? ...

If all things were eternal,
And nothing their end bringing,
If this should be then how should we
Here make an end of singing?

ANON

Ducks Don't Shop in Sainsbury's

YOU can't get millet at Sainsbury's
and they don't sell grass or weed
it's a total dead loss
for heather and moss
and they don't stock sunflower seed.

They've got some fish in the freezer
but they're low on rats and mice
and you're out of luck
if you're a debonair duck
and you want to buy something nice

'cos none of their bread is stale
and they've stopped selling hay and straw.
Let's face it, if you were a duck in Sainsbury's,
you'd be heading for the exit door!

GARY BOSWELL (1960-)

Three Young Rats

THREE young rats with black felt hats,
  Three young ducks with white straw flats,
    Three young dogs with curling tails,
     Three young cats with demi-veils,
        Went out to walk with two young pigs
        In satin vests and sorrel wigs;
          But suddenly it chanced to rain,
          And so they all went home again.

ANON

Two Limericks about Clothes

THERE was a young man of Bengal
Who went to a fancy-dress ball.
    He went just for fun
    Dressed up as a bun,
And a dog ate him up in the hall.

THERE was an old person of Fratton
Who would go to church with his hat on,
    'If I wake up,' he said,
    'With my hat on my head,
I shall know that it hasn't been sat on.'

ANON

An Elegy on the Death of a Mad Dog

GOOD people all, of every sort,
    Give ear unto my song;
And if you find it wondrous short,
    It cannot hold you long.
In Islington there was a man,
    Of whom the world might say,
That still a godly race he ran,
    Whene'er he went to pray …
And in that town a dog was found,
    As many dogs there be,
Both mongrel, puppy, whelp, and hound,
    And curs of low degree.
This dog and man at first were friends;
    But when a pique began,
The dog, to gain some private ends,
    Went mad and bit the man …
The wound it seemed both sore and sad
    To every Christian eye;
And while they swore the dog was mad,
    They swore the man would die.
But soon a wonder came to light,
    That showed the rogues they lied:
The man recover'd of the bite—
    The dog it was that died.

OLIVER GOLDSMITH (?1730-1774)

Engraved on the Collar of a Dog, which I gave to His Royal Highness

I AM his Highness' dog at Kew;
Pray tell me, sir, whose dog are you?

ALEXANDER POPE (1688-1744)

Two Limericks about Misunderstanding

THERE was an old man from Darjeeling,
Who boarded a bus bound for Ealing.
       He saw on the door:
       'Please don't spit on the floor',
So he stood up and spat on the ceiling.

THERE was an old fellow of Tring
Who, when somebody asked him to sing,
       Replied, 'Ain't it odd?
       I can never tell God
Save the Weasel from Pop goes the King.'

ANON

Limerick about Corks

THERE was an old waiter from Wapping,
Drew corks for a week without stopping;
    Cried he, 'It's too bad!
    The practice I've had!
Yet cannot prevent them from popping.'

WALTER PARKE

How Doth the Little Crocodile

HOW doth the little crocodile
  Improve his shining tail,
And pour the waters of the Nile
  On every golden scale!

How cheerfully he seems to grin,
  How neatly spreads his claws,
And welcomes little fishes in,
  With gently smiling jaws!

LEWIS CARROLL (1832-1898)

Hippopotamus Song

A BOLD Hippopotamus was standing one day
On the banks of the cool Shalimar.
He gazed at the bottom as it peacefully lay
By the light of the evening star.
Away on a hilltop sat combing her hair
His fair Hippopotamine maid;
The Hippopotamus was no ignoramus
And sang her this sweet serenade.

    Mud, Mud, glorious mud,
      Nothing quite like it for cooling the blood!
    So follow me, follow
    Down to the hollow
    And there let us wallow
    In glorious mud! …

Now more Hippopotami began to convene
On the banks of that river so wide.
I wonder now what am I to say of the scene
That ensued by the Shalimar side?
They dived all at once with an ear-splitting splosh
Then rose to the surface again,
A regular army of Hippopotami
All singing this haunting refrain.

    Mud! Mud! Glorious mud! …

MICHAEL FLANDERS (1922-1975)

The Octopus

TELL me, O Octopus, I begs,
Is those things arms, or is they legs?
I marvel at thee, Octopus;
If I were thou, I'd call me Us.

OGDEN NASH (1902-1971)

The Lobster-Quadrille

'WILL you walk a little faster?' said a whiting to a snail,
'There's a porpoise close behind us, and he's treading on
    my tail.
See how eagerly the lobsters and the turtles all advance!
They are waiting on the shingle—will you come and join
    the dance?
       Will you, won't you, will you, won't you, will you
          join the dance?
       Will you, won't you, will you, won't you, won't you
          join the dance?

'You can really have no notion how delightful it will be
When they take us up and throw us, with the lobsters, out
    to sea!'
But the snail replied 'Too far, too far!' and gave a look
    askance—
Said he thanked the whiting kindly, but he would not join
    the dance.
       Would not, could not, would not, could not, would
          not join the dance.
       Would not, could not, would not, could not, could
          not join the dance …

LEWIS CARROLL (1832-1898)

The Walrus

THE Walrus lives on icy floes
And unsuspecting Eskimoes.

Don't bring your wife to Arctic Tundra
A Walrus may bob up from undra.

MICHAEL FLANDERS (1922-1975)

The Man in the Wilderness

THE man in the wilderness asked of me,
How many strawberries grow in the sea?
I answered him as I thought good,
As many red herrings as grow in the wood.

ANON

The Pig

'TWAS an evening in November,
As I very well remember,
I was strolling down the street in drunken pride,
But my knees were all aflutter,
So I landed in the gutter,
And a pig came up and lay down by my side.

Yes, I lay there in the gutter
Thinking thoughts I could not utter,
When a lady passing by did softly say,
'Ye can tell a man that boozes
By the company he chooses.'—
At that the pig got up and walked away!

ANON

The Mule and the Horse

THE MULE

MY MAMMY was a wall-eyed goat,
My Old Man was an ass,
And I feed myself off leather boots
And dynamite and grass;
For I'm a mule, a long-eared fool
And I ain't never been to school—
    Mammeee! Ma-ha-mam-hee!
    Heee-haw! Mamaah!
    Ma-ha-mee!

THE HORSE

I KNOW two things about the horse,
And one of them is rather coarse.

ANON

The Rabbit

THE rabbit has a charming face:
Its private life is a disgrace.
I really dare not name to you
The awful things that rabbits do;
Things that your paper never prints—
You only mention them in hints.
They have such lost, degraded souls
No wonder they inhabit holes;
When such depravity is found
It only can live underground.

ANON

Two Clerihews about Ancient Rome

THE Empress Poppaea
Was really rather a dear,
Only no one could stop her
From being improper.

THE Emperor Arcadius
Lived outside the four-mile radius,
Which made it rather laborious
To visit the Emperor Honorius.

ANON

Two Clerihews about Famous Authors

GEOFFREY Chaucer
Always drank out of a saucer.
He said it made him feel such an ass
To drink out of a glass.

JONATHAN Swift
Never went up in a lift;
Nor did the author of 'Robinson Crusoe'
Do so.

ANON

A Case

AS I was going up the stair
I met a man who wasn't there.
He wasn't there again today—
I wish to God he'd go away!

ANON

The Dolgelley Hotel

IF EVER you go to Dolgelley,
    Don't stay at the ——— HOTEL;
There's nothing to put in your belly,
    And no-one to answer the bell.

THOMAS HUGHES (1822-1896)

A Motorway Nursery Rhyme

MARY, Mary, quite contrary,
　　Why do you drive so slow?
Oh, I try to annoy other drivers
　　As on my way I go.

I flash my indicator
　　And then I don't pull out
Which tends to create in others
　　An element of doubt.

When someone else is passing
　　I like to accelerate
And then they can't get past me—
　　That's something they all hate.

Mary, Mary, quite contrary,
　　How do you drive your car?
Oh, I drive it very slowly
　　And I drive it very far.

MILES KINGTON (1941-)

The Modern Hiawatha

HE KILLED the noble Mudjokivis.
Of the skin he made him mittens,
Made them with the fur side inside,
Made them with the skin side outside.
He, to get the warm side inside,
Put the inside skin side outside;
He, to get the cold side outside,
Put the warm side fur side inside.
That's why he put the fur side inside,
Why he put the skin side outside,
Why he turned them inside outside.

GEORGE A STRONG (1832-1912)

Hiawatha's Photographing

FROM his shoulder Hiawatha
Took the camera of rosewood,
Made of sliding, folding rosewood;
Neatly put it all together …
She came dressed beyond description,
Dressed in jewels and in satin
Far too gorgeous for an empress.
Gracefully she sat down sideways,
With a simper scarcely human,
Holding in her hand a bouquet
Rather larger than a cabbage.
All the while that she was sitting,
Still the lady chattered, chattered,
Like a monkey in the forest.
'Am I sitting still?' she asked him.
'Is my face enough in profile?
Shall I hold the nosegay higher?
Will it come into the picture?'
And the picture failed completely …

LEWIS CARROLL (1832-1898)

A True Maid

'NO, NO; for my virginity,
    When I lose that,' says Rose, 'I'll die':
'Behind the elms last night,' cried Dick,
    'Rose, were you not extremely sick?'

MATTHEW PRIOR (1664-1721)

On Taking a Wife

'COME, come,' said Tom's father, 'at your time of life,
 There's no longer excuse for thus playing the rake.
It's time you should think, boy, of taking a wife.'
 'Why so it is, father. Whose wife shall I take?'

THOMAS MOORE (1779-1852)

Roger and Dolly

YOUNG Roger came tapping at Dolly's window,
    Tumpaty, tumpaty, tump.
He begged for admittance, she answered him, 'No',
    Glumpaty, glumpaty, glump.
'My Dolly, my dear, your true love is here',
    Dumpaty, dumpaty, dump.
'No, Roger, no, as you came you may go',
    Clumpaty, clumpaty, clump.

'O what is the reason, dear Dolly,' he cried,
    Pumpaty, pumpaty, pump.
'That thus I'm cast off and unkindly denied?'
    Frumpaty, frumpaty, frump.
'Some rival more dear I guess has been here',
    Crumpaty, crumpaty, crump.
'Suppose there's been two; pray, sir, what's that to you?'
    Numpaty, numpaty, nump.

O then with a sigh a sad farewell he took,
    Lumpaty, lumpaty, lump.
And all in despair he leaped into the brook,
    Flumpaty, flumpaty, flump.
His courage it cooled, he found himself fooled,
    Trumpaty, trumpaty, trump.
He swam to the shore and saw Dolly no more,
    Rumpaty, rumpaty, rump …

HENRY CAREY (?-1743)

A Lunatic's Love Song

O, KNOW you the land where the cheese-tree grows,
And the unicorn spins on the end of his nose;
Where the sea-mew scowls on the circling bat,
And the elephant hunts in an opera hat?

'Tis there that I lie with my head in a pond,
And play with a valueless Tichborne bond;
'Tis there that I sip pure Horniman's tea
To the sound of the gong and the howling sea.

'Tis there that I revel in soapsuds and rum,
And wait till my creditors choose to come;
'Tis there that I dream of the days when I
Shall soar to the moon through the red-hot sky.

Then come, oh come to that happy land!
And don't forget your galvanic band;
We will play at cards in the lion's den,
And go to bed when the clock strikes ten.

ANON

St Ives

AS I was going to St Ives
I met a man with seven wives.
Said he, 'I think it's much more fun
Than getting stuck with only one.'

ROALD DAHL (1916-90)

Matrimony

'TIS an act of the priest to give patience a test;
'Tis a desperate hope, and a serious jest;
'Tis catching a dolt, when his wit is suspended;
'Tis a toil, where the labour can never be ended;
'Tis a leap in the dark, which both parties agree
To perform hand in hand, though they neither can see;
'Tis walking through mines filled with sulphurous vapour,
Where to find out a path, you must brandish a taper;
'Tis like Tantalus' feast, where the good does but seem,
And both ope their eyes, though they're both in a dream;
'Tis going to sea, in a black stormy night,
Which reason calls madness, but custom delight:
For Wedlock's a minx who deceives by her sleekness,
As Craft wove a cloak to envelop her weakness.
'Tis a comical, tragical, fiery ordeal,
Where the ploughshares are hot, and your faith is not real.

JOHN WILLIAMS (1761-1818)

One Perfect Rose

A SINGLE flow'r he sent me, since we met.
All tenderly his messenger he chose;
Deep-hearted, pure, with scented dew still wet—
One perfect rose.

I knew the language of the floweret;
'My fragile leaves,' it said, 'his heart enclose.'
Love long has taken for his amulet
One perfect rose.

Why is it no one ever sent me yet
One perfect limousine, do you suppose?
Ah no, it's always just my luck to get
One perfect rose.

DOROTHY PARKER (1893-1967)

Limerick about Wives

THERE was an old party of Lyme
Who married three wives at one time.
　　When asked: 'Why the third?'
　　He replied, 'One's absurd,
And bigamy, sir, is a crime.'

ANON

Susan Simpson

SUDDEN swallows swiftly skimming,
    Sunset's slowly spreading shade,
Silvery songsters sweetly singing
    Summer's soothing serenade.

Susan Simpson strolled sedately,
    Stifling sobs, suppressing sighs.
Seeing Stephen Slocum, stately
    She stopped, showing some surprise.

'Say', said Stephen, 'sweetest sigher;
    Say, shall Stephen spouseless stay?'
Susan, seeming somewhat shyer,
    Showed submissiveness straightway.

Summer's season slowly stretches,
    Susan Simpson Slocum she—
So she signed some simple sketches—
    Soul sought soul successfully.

Six Septembers Susan swelters;
    Six sharp seasons snow supplies;
Susan's satin sofa shelters
    Six small Slocums side by side.

ANON

Maternal Despotism; or, The Rights of Infants

UNHAND me nurse! Thou saucy quean!
What does this female tyrant mean?
Thus, head and foot, in swathes to bind,
'Spite of the 'Rights of human kind';
And lay me stretched upon my back
(Like a poor culprit on the rack);
An infant, like thyself born free,
And independent, slut! on thee.

    Have I not right to kick and sprawl,
To laugh or cry, to squeak or squall!
Has ever, by my act and deed,
Thy *right* to rule me been decreed?
How dar'st thou, despot! then control
Th' exertions of a free-born soul?

    Though now an infant, when I can,
I'll rise and seize 'The Rights of Man';
Nor make my haughty nurse alone,
But monarchs tremble, on their throne;
And boys and kings thenceforth you'll see
Enjoy complete *Equality*.

RICHARD GRAVES (1715-1804)

A Parental Ode to My Son, aged Three Years and Five Months

　　THOU happy, happy elf!
(But stop—first let me kiss away that tear)—
　　Thou tiny image of myself!
(My love, he's poking peas into his ear!)
Thou merry, laughing sprite!
With spirits feather-light,
Untouch'd by sorrow, and unsoil'd by sin—
(Good heavens! the child is swallowing a pin!)

　　Thou little tricksy Puck!
With antic toys so funnily bestuck,
Light as the singing bird that wings the air—
(The door! the door! he'll tumble down the stair!)
　　Thou darling of thy sire!
(Why, Jane, he'll set his pinafore a-fire!)
　　Thou imp of mirth and joy!
In Love's dear chain so strong and bright a link,
Thou idol of thy parents—(drat the boy!
　　　　there goes my ink!) ...

THOMAS HOOD (1799-1845)

The Twins

IN FORM and feature, face and limb,
    I grew so like my brother,
That folks got taking me for him
    And each for one another.
It puzzled all our kith and kin,
    It reach'd an awful pitch;
For one of us was born a twin
    And not a soul knew which.

One day (to make the matter worse),
    Before our names were fix'd,
As we were being washed by nurse
    We got completely mix'd;
And thus, you see, by Fate's decree
    (Or rather nurse's whim)
My brother John got christened *me*,
    And I got christened *him* ...

Our close resemblance turned the tide
    Of my domestic life;
For somehow my intended bride
    Became my brother's wife.
In short, year after year the same
    Absurd mistakes went on;
And when I died—the neighbours came
    And buried brother John!

HENRY SAMBROOKE LEIGH (1837-1883)

Sartorial Solecism

POOR Uncle Joe
Can't help his face,
But what I wished to know
Was why he must all disgrace
By wearing a thing so out of place
As a bowler-hat for sailing!

Said Auntie Flo:
'It may not be
Quite the thing to wear at sea,
But look how well it softens the blow
When the boom swings over on Uncle Joe!
Besides, it's grand for bailing.'

R E C STRINGER

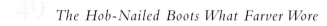

The Hob-Nailed Boots What Farver Wore

MY FARVER'S feet filled up arf a street
So his boots was in proportion,
And the kids he'd squash in a week, by gosh!
It really was a caution.
Well, me and me bruvvers at the age of four,
All wrapped up cosy in a box of straw,
Till eleven in the morning used to sleep and snore,
In the hob-nailed boots what farver wore.

When Madge and Flo went to Southend, so
As money they'd be saving
Father's boots were seen as a bathin' machine
Where the bathers 'ud change for bathin'.
Well, while they was changin', they forgot, I'm sure,
The hole he had cut for his corns, and cor!
The boys started giggling at what they saw—
In the hob-nailed boots what farver wore …

ANON

Hunter Trials

IT'S awf'lly bad luck on Diana,
    Her ponies have swallowed their bits;
She fished down their throats with a spanner
    And frightened them all into fits ...

Just look at Prunella on Guzzle,
    The wizardest pony on earth;
Why doesn't she slacken his muzzle
    And tighten the breech in his girth? ...

And Margaret failed in her paces,
    Her withers got tied in a noose,
So her coronets caught in the traces
    And now all her fetlocks are loose.

Oh, it's me now. I'm terribly nervous.
    I wonder if Smudges will shy.
She's practically certain to swerve as
    Her Pelham is over one eye.

Oh wasn't it naughty of Smudges?
    Oh, Mummy, I'm sick with disgust.
She threw me in front of the Judges,
    And my silly old collarbone's bust.

SIR JOHN BETJEMAN (1906-1984)

There Was a Naughty Boy

THERE was a naughty Boy,
   And a naughty Boy was he,
He ran away to Scotland
   The people for to see—

      Then he found
      That the ground
      Was as hard,
      That a yard
      Was as long,
      That a song
      Was as merry,
      That a cherry
      Was as red—
      That lead
      Was as weighty,
      That fourscore
      Was as eighty,
      That a door
      Was as wooden
      As in England—

So he stood in his shoes
   And he wonder'd,
    He wonder'd,
He stood in his shoes
   And he wonder'd.

JOHN KEATS (1795-1821)

The Freshman's Soliloquy

I WONDER who that man can be
Now coming near! He seems to me
Like one who holds within his hand
The sun, the moon, the planets, and
Maintains this little world of ours
Obedient to his sovereign powers.
What stately mien and look has he,
Compared with men of less degree!
That must be 'Prex,' or some great Prof.—
I think I'll take my hat quite off.

  [A Voice.]
Oh, no, young sir,
You greatly err!
 It is the college carpenter.

OZORA STEARNS DAVIS (1866-1931)

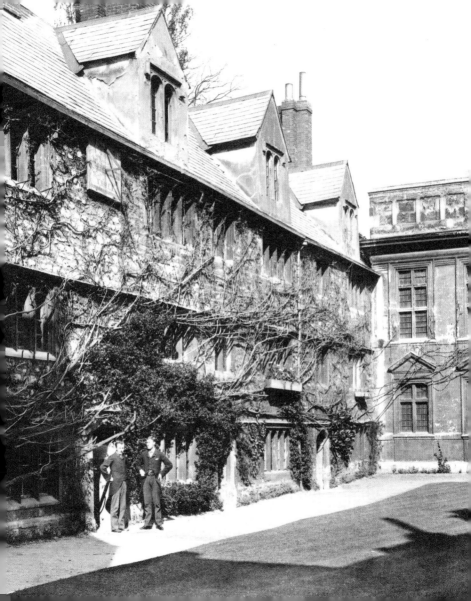

Wishes of an Elderly Man at a Garden Party

I WISH I loved the human race;
I wish I loved its silly face;
I wish I liked the way it walks;
I wish I liked the way it talks;
And when I'm introduced to one
I wish I thought *What Jolly Fun!*

WALTER RALEIGH (1861-1922)

The Last Decalogue

THOU shalt have one God only; who
Would be at the expense of two?
No graven images may be
Worshipped, except the currency:
Swear not at all; for, for thy curse
Thine enemy is none the worse:
At church on Sunday to attend
Will serve to keep the world thy friend:
Honour thy parents; that is, all
From whom advancement may befall:
Thou shalt not kill; but need'st not strive
Officiously to keep alive:
Do not adultery commit;
Advantage rarely comes of it:
Thou shalt not steal; an empty feat,
When it's so lucrative to cheat:
Bear not false witness; let the lie
Have time on its own wings to fly:
Thou shalt not covet, but tradition
Approves all forms of competition.

ARTHUR HUGH CLOUGH (1819-1861)

from The Pirates of Penzance:
The Policeman's Lot

WHEN a felon's not engaged in his employment,
    Or maturing his felonious little plans,
His capacity for innocent enjoyment
    Is just as great as any honest man's.
Our feelings we with difficulty smother
    When constabulary duty's to be done:
Ah, take one consideration with another,
    A policeman's lot is not a happy one!

When the enterprising burglar isn't burgling,
    When the cut-throat isn't occupied in crime,
He loves to hear the little brook a-gurgling,
    And listen to the merry village chime.
When the coster's finished jumping on his mother,
    He loves to lie a-basking in the sun:
Ah, take one consideration with another,
    The policeman's lot is not a happy one!

W S GILBERT (1836-1911)

Sergeant Brown's Parrot

MANY policemen wear upon their shoulders
Cunning little radios. To pass away the time
They talk about the traffic to them, listen to the news.
And it helps them to Keep Down Crime.

But Sergeant Brown, he wears upon his shoulder
A tall green parrot as he's walking up and down,
And all the parrot says is 'Who's-a-pretty-boy-then?'
'I am,' says Sergeant Brown.

KIT WRIGHT (1944-)

Lord Heygate and Lord Finchley

LORD Heygate had a troubled face,
His furniture was commonplace—
The sort of Peer who well might pass
For someone of the middle class.
I do not think you want to hear
About this unimportant Peer.

LORD Finchley tried to mend the Electric Light
Himself. It struck him dead: And serve him right!
It is the business of the wealthy man
To give employment to the artisan.

HILAIRE BELLOC (1870-1953)

Lord Gorbals

ONCE, as old Lord Gorbals motored
   Round his moors near John o' Groats,
He collided with a goatherd
   And a herd of forty goats.
By the time his car got through
They were all defunct but two.

Roughly he addressed the goatherd:
   'Dash my whiskers and my corns!
Can't you teach your goats, you dotard,
   That they ought to sound their horns?
Look, my A.A. badge is bent!
I've a mind to raise your rent!'

HARRY GRAHAM (1874-1936)

from Iolanthe: The Lord Chancellors' Song

WHEN I went to the Bar as a very young man,
    (Said I to myself—said I),
I'll work on a new and original plan,
    (Said I to myself—said I),
I'll never assume that a rogue or a thief
Is a gentleman worthy implicit belief,
Because his attorney has sent me a brief,
    (Said I to myself—said I!)

Ere I go into court I will read my brief through
    (Said I to myself—said I),
And I'll never take work I'm unable to do
    (Said I to myself-said I),
My learned profession I'll never disgrace
By taking a fee with a grin on my face,
When I haven't been there to attend to the case
    (Said I to myself—said I!)

I'll never throw dust in a juryman's eyes
    (Said I to myself—said I),
Or hoodwink a judge who is not over-wise
    (Said I to myself—said I),
Or assume that the witnesses summoned in force
In Exchequer, Queen's Bench, Common Pleas, or
    Divorce,
Have perjured themselves as a matter of course
    (Said I to myself—said I!) ...

W S GILBERT (1836-1911)

Election Time

GATHER ye bank-notes while ye may;
  The happy time is flitting;
The Member canvassing today
  Tomorrow will be sitting.

That glorious crib, the Rising Sun,
  Where patriots are glowing,
Too soon its brilliant course is run,
  Its beer will soon stop flowing.

ANON

Much Ado About Nothing in the City

SIGH no more, dealers, sigh no more,
    Shares were unstable ever,
They often have been down before,
    At high rates constant never.
        Then sigh not so,
        Soon up they'll go,
And you'll be blithe and funny,
    Converting all your notes of woe
Into hey money, money.

Write no more letters, write no mo
    On stocks so dull and heavy.
At times on 'Change 'tis always so,
    When bears a tribute levy.
        Then sigh not so,
        And don't be low,
In sunshine you'll make honey,
    Converting all your notes of woe
Into hey money, money.

ANON

from HMS Pinafore: Sir Joseph Porter's Song

WHEN I was a lad I served a term
As office boy to an Attorney's firm.
I cleaned the windows and I swept the floor,
And I polished up the handle of the big front door.
    I polished up that handle so carefullee
    That now I am the Ruler of the Queen's Navee! ...

Of legal knowledge I acquired such a grip
That they took me into the partnership.
And that junior partnership, I ween,
Was the only ship that I ever had seen.
    But that kind of ship so suited me,
    That now I am the Ruler of the Queen's Navee!

I grew so rich that I was sent
By a pocket borough into Parliament.
I always voted at my party's call,
And I never thought of thinking for myself at all.
    I thought so little, they rewarded me
    By making me the Ruler of the Queen's Navee!

Now landsmen all, whoever you may be,
If you want to rise to the top of the tree,
If your soul isn't fettered to an office stool,
Be careful to be guided by this golden rule—
    Stick close to your desks and never go to sea,
    And you all may be rulers of the Queen's Navee!

W S GILBERT (1836-1911)

Limerick about a Boat

THERE was an Old Man in a boat,
Who said, 'I'm afloat! I'm afloat!'
    When they said, 'No! you ain't!'
    He was ready to faint,
That unhappy old man in a boat.

EDWARD LEAR (1812-1888)

The Fleas

GREAT fleas have little fleas upon their backs to bite 'em,
And little fleas have lesser fleas and so ad infinitum.
And the great fleas themselves, in turn, have greater fleas to
    go on;
While these again have greater still, and greater still, and
    so on.

A DE MORGAN (1806-1871)

Gasbags

I'M THANKFUL that the sun and moon
Are both hung up so high
That no pretentious hand can stretch
And pull them from the sky.
If they were not, I have no doubt,
But some reforming ass
Would recommend to take them down
And light the world with gas.

ANON

The Handkerchief Ghost

THERE is a ghost
That eats handkerchiefs;
It keeps you company
On all your travels, and
Eats your handkerchiefs
Out of your trunk, your
Bed, your washstand,
Like a bird eating
Out of your hand, —not
All of them and not
All at one go. With
Eighteen handkerchiefs
You set out, a proud mariner,
On the seas of the Unknown;
With eight or perhaps
Seven you come back, the
Despair of the housewife.

CHRISTIAN MORGENSTERN
TRANSLATED BY R F C HULL

The Stately Homes of England

THE stately homes of England, how beautiful they stand—
To prove the upper classes have still the upper hand;
Tho' the fact that they have to be rebuilt
And frequently mortgag'd to the hilt
Is inclin'd to take the gilt off the gingerbread,
And certainly damps the fun,
Of the eldest son—
But still we won't be beaten,
We'll scrimp and screw and save—
The playing fields of Eton have made us frightfully brave—
And tho' if the Van Dycks have to go
And we pawn the Bechstein grand,
We'll stand by the stately homes of England! ...

The stately homes of England, tho' rather in the lurch,
Provide a lot of chances for psychical research:
There's a ghost of a crazy younger son,
Who murder'd in thirteen fifty-one
An extremely rowdy nun (who resented it),
And people who come to call
Meet her in the hall.
The baby in the guest wing who crouches by the grate
Was wall'd up in the west wing in fourteen twenty-eight.
And if anyone spots the Queen of Scots in a hand-
    embroider'd shroud,
We're proud of the stately homes of England.

NÖEL COWARD (1899-1973)

How to Get On in Society

PHONE for the fish-knives, Norman
　　As Cook is a little unnerved;
You kiddies have crumpled the serviettes
　　And I must have things daintily served.

Are the requisites all in the toilet?
　　The frills round the cutlets can wait
Till the girl has replenished the cruets
　　And switched on the logs in the grate.

It's ever so close in the lounge, dear,
　　But the vestibule's comfy for tea
And Howard is out riding on horseback
　　So do come and take some with me.

Now here is a fork for your pastries
　　And do use the couch for your feet;
I know that I wanted to ask you—
　　Is trifle sufficient for sweet?

Milk and then just as it comes dear?
　　I'm afraid the preserve's full of stones;
Beg pardon, I'm soiling the doileys
　　With afternoon tea-cakes and scones.

JOHN BETJEMAN (1906-1984)

Peas

I ALWAYS eat peas with honey,
I've done it all my life,
They do taste kind of funny
But it keeps them on the knife.

ANON

Limerick about the Clergy

THERE was an Archdeacon who said:
'May I take off my gaiters in bed?'
     But the Bishop said: 'No,
     Wherever you go
You must wear them until you are dead.'

ANON

The Village Choir

HALF a bar, half a bar,
Half a bar onward!
Into an awful ditch
Choir and precentor hitch,
Into a mess of pitch
    They led the Old Hundred.
Trebles to right of them,
Tenors to left of them,
Basses in front of them,
    Bellowed and thundered.
Oh, that precentor's look,
When the sopranos took
Their own time and hook
    From the Old Hundred!

Screeched all the trebles here,
Boggled the tenors there,
Raising the parson's hair,
    While his mind wandered;
Theirs not to reason why
This psalm was pitched too high:
Theirs but to gasp and cry
    Out the Old Hundred ...

ANON

Swans Sing Before They Die

SWANS sing before they die—'twere no bad thing
Should certain persons die before they sing.

SAMUEL TAYLOR COLERIDGE (1772-1834)

Our Pond

I AM fond
Of our pond,
Of the superfine gloss
On its moss,
Its pink lilies and things
And the wings
    Of its duck.

I am keen
On the green
Soupy surface of some
Of its scum,
Its water-waved weeds,
Its three reeds
    And its muck.

Yesterday,
As I lay
And admired its thick skin,
I fell in;
I went walloping down
    Till I stuck.

I am fond
Of our pond,
But I like it much more
From the shore.
It was quite out of place
On my face,
     Where it stuck.

DANIEL PETTIWARD

Two Limericks about Eccentricity

THERE was an old man from Dunoon,
Who always ate soup with a fork,
      For he said, 'As I eat
      Neither fish, fowl nor flesh,
I should finish my dinner too quick.'

THERE was an old loony of Lyme,
Whose candour was simply sublime;
      When they asked, 'Are you there?'
      'Yes,' he said, 'but take care,
For I'm never "all there" at a time.'

ANON

To the Moon

OH MOON, when I look on thy beautiful face,
Careering along through the boundaries of space,
The thought has quite frequently come to my mind,
If ever I'll gaze on thy glorious behind.

ANON

Belagcholly Days

CHILLY Dovebber with his boadigg blast
    Dow cubs add strips the bedow add the lawd,
Eved October's suddy days are past—
        Add Subber's gawd!

I kdow dot what it is to which I cligg
    That stirs to sogg add sorrow, yet I trust
That still I sigg, but as the liddets sigg—
        Because I bust.

Add now, farewell to roses add to birds,
    To larded fields and tigkligg streablets eke;
Farewell to all articulated words
        I fain would speak.

Farewell, by cherished strolliggs od the sward,
    Greed glades and forest shades, farewell to you;
With sorrowing heart I, wretched add forlord,
        Bid you—achew!!!

ANON

No!

NO SUN—no moon!
No morn—no noon—
No dawn—no dusk—no proper time of day—
No sky—no earthly view—
No distance looking blue—
No road—no street—no 't'other side the way'—
No end to any Row—
No indications where the Crescents go—
No top to any steeple—
No recognitions of familiar people—
No courtesies for showing 'em!—
No knowing 'em!—
No travelling at all—no locomotion,
No inkling of the way—no notion—
'No go'—by land or ocean—
No mail—no post—
No news from any foreign coast—
No Park—no Ring—no afternoon gentility—
No company—no nobility—
No warmth, no cheerfulness, no healthful ease,
No comfortable feel in any member—
No shade, no shine, no butterflies, no bees,
No fruits, no flow'rs, no leaves, no birds—
November!

THOMAS HOOD (1799-1845)

Weather Forecast

THE rain it raineth every day,
Upon the just and unjust fella,
But more upon the just, because
The unjust has the just's umbrella.

ANON

Watch Your Step—I'm Drenched

IN MANCHESTER there are a thousand puddles.
Bus-queue puddles poised on slanting paving stones,
Railway puddles slouching outside stations,
Cinema puddles in ambush at the exits,
Zebra-crossing puddles in dips of the dark stripes—
They lurk in the murk
Of the north-western evening
For the sake of their notorious joke,
Their only joke—to soak
The tights or trousers of the citizens.
Each splash and consequent curse is echoed by
One thousand dark Mancunian puddle chuckles.

In Manchester there lives the King of Puddles,
Master of Miniature Muck Lakes,
The Shah of Slosh, Splendifero of Splash,
Prince, Pasha and Pope of Puddledom.
Where? Somewhere. The rain-headed ruler
Lies doggo, incognito,
Disguised as an average, accidental mini-pool.
He is as scared as any other emperor,
For one night, all his soiled and soggy victims
Might storm his streets, assassination in their minds,
A thousand rolls of blotting paper in their hands,
And drink his shadowed, one-joke life away.

ADRIAN MITCHELL (1932-)

The Twelve Months

SNOWY, Flowy, Blowy,
Showery, Flowery, Bowery,
Hoppy, Croppy, Droppy,
Breezy, Sneezy, Freezy.

GEORGE ELLIS (1753-1815)

No Doctors Today, Thank You

THEY tell me that euphoria is the feeling of feeling
    wonderful; well, today I feel euphorian,
Today I have the agility of a Greek God and the appetite of
    a Victorian,
Yes, today I may even go forth without my galoshes;
Today I am a swashbuckler, would anybody like me to
    buckle my swashes?
This is my euphorian day.
I will ring welkins and before anybody answers I will run
    away …
I will pen me my memoirs.
Ah, youth, youth! What euphorian days them was!
I wasn't much of a hand for the boudoirs,
I was generally to be found where the food was.
Does anybody want any flotsam?
I've gotsam.
Does anybody want any jetsam?
I can getsam.
I can play 'Chopsticks' on the Wurlitzer,
I can speak Portuguese like a Berlitzer.
I can don or doff my shoes without tying or untying the
    laces because I am wearing moccasins,
And I practically know the difference between serums and
    anti-toccasins.
Kind people, don't think me purse-proud, don't set me
    down as vainglorious,
I'm just a little euphorious.

OGDEN NASH (1902-1971)

Peekaboo, I almost See You

MIDDLE-AGED life is merry, and I love to lead it,
But there comes a day when your eyes are all right, but your
    arm isn't long enough to hold the telephone book
    where you can read it,
And your friends get jocular, so you go to the oculist,
And of all your friends he is the joculist,
So over his facetiousness let us skim,
Only noting that he has been waiting for you ever since you
    said Good Evening to his grandfather clock under the
    impression that it was him.
And you look at his chart and it says SHRDLU
    QWERTYOP, and you say Well, why SHRDNTLU
    QWERTYOP? and he says one set of glasses won't do.
You need two,
One for reading Erle Stanley Gardner's Perry Mason and
    Keats's 'Endymion' with,
And the other for walking around without saying Hallo to
    strange wymion with,
So you spend your time taking off your seeing glasses to put
    on your reading glasses, and then remembering that
    your reading glasses are upstairs or in the car,
And then you can't find your seeing glasses again because
    without them you can't see where they are.

Enough of such mishaps, they would try the patience of
     an ox,
I prefer to forget both pairs of glasses and pass my declining
     years saluting strange women and grandfather clocks.

OGDEN NASH (1902-1971)

In the Arms of My Glasses

THEY can call me softy
as ofty
as they please
but still I'll stand by these
my little optical accessories
they stop me walking into lampposts
and trees
when it's foggy
and I'm out walking with my doggie

JOHN HEGLEY (1953-)

On Dr Isaac Letsome

WHEN people's ill they comes to I,
    I physics, bleeds, and sweats 'em,
Sometimes they live, sometimes they die;
    What's that to I? I Letsome.

ANON

from Iolanthe: The Lord Chancellor's Song

WHEN you're lying awake with a dismal headache, and
      repose is taboo'd by anxiety,
I conceive you may use any language you choose to indulge
      in, without impropriety;
For your brain is on fire—the bedclothes conspire of usual
      slumber to plunder you:
First your counterpane goes, and uncovers your toes, and
      your sheet slips demurely from under you;
Then the blanketing tickles—you feel like mixed pickles—
      so terribly sharp is the pricking,
And you're hot, and you're cross, and you tumble and toss
      till there's nothing 'twixt you and the ticking.
Then the bedclothes all creep to the ground in a heap, and
      you pick 'em all up in a tangle;
Next your pillow resigns and politely declines to remain at
      its usual angle!
Well, you get some repose in the form of a doze, with hot
      eye-balls and head ever aching.
But your slumbering teems with such horrible dreams that
      you'd very much better be waking …

W S GILBERT (1836-1911)

Oh, I Wish I'd Looked After Me Teeth

OH, I wish I'd looked after me teeth,
   And spotted the perils beneath,
All the toffees I chewed,
   And the sweet sticky food.
Oh, I wish I'd looked after me teeth …

When I think of the lollies I licked,
   And the liquorice allsorts I picked,
Sherbet dabs, big and little,
   All that hard peanut brittle,
My conscience gets horribly pricked …

So I lay in the old dentist's chair,
   And I gaze up his nose in despair,
And his drill it do whine,
   In these molars of mine,
'Two amalgam,' he'll say, 'for in there.'

How I laughed at my mother's false teeth,
   As they foamed in the waters beneath,
But now comes the reckonin'
It's *me* they are beckonin'
   Oh, I *wish* I'd looked after me teeth.

PAM AYRES (1947-)

Two Limericks about Health

THERE was a faith-healer of Deal,
Who said, 'Although pain isn't real,
    If I sit on a pin
    And it punctures my skin,
I dislike what I fancy I feel.'

THERE was a young lady of Spain
Who was dreadfully sick in a train,
    Not once, but again,
    And again and again,
And again and again and again.

ANON

Two Ruthless Rhymes

OPPORTUNITY

WHEN Mrs Gorm (Aunt Eloïse)
Was stung to death by savage bees,
Her husband (Prebendary Gorm)
Put on his veil, and took the swarm.
He's publishing a book next May
On 'How to Make Bee-Keeping Pay'.

MR JONES

'THERE'S been an accident,' they said,
'Your servant's cut in half; he's dead!'
'Indeed!' said Mr Jones, 'and please,
Send me the half that's got my keys.'

HARRY GRAHAM (1874-1936)

Two Limericks about Death

A SIMPLE young fellow named Hyde
In a funeral procession was spied.
   When asked, 'Who is dead?'
   He tittered and said,
'I don't know. I just came for the ride.'

THERE was an old man of Khartoum
Who kept a tame sheep in his room.
   'To remind me', he said,
   'Of someone who's dead,
But I never can recollect whom'.

ANON

Burlesque of Lope de Vega

IF THE man who turnips cries,
Cry not when his father dies,
'Tis a proof that he had rather
Have a turnip than his father.

SAMUEL JOHNSON (1709-1784)

Epitaph on Prince Frederick

HERE lies Fred,
Who was alive and is dead.
Had it been his father,
I had much rather;
Had it been his brother,
Still better than another;
Had it been his sister,
No one would have miss'd her;
Had it been the whole generation,
Still better for the nation;
But since 'tis only Fred,
Who was alive and is dead,
There's no more to be said.

ANON

Epitaph

HERE lie I and my four daughters,
Killed by drinking Cheltenham waters.
Had we but stuck to Epsom salts,
We wouldn't have been in these here vaults.

ANON

93 *On Visiting Westminster Abbey*

HOLY Moses! Have a look!
Flesh decayed in every nook!
Some rare bits of brain be here
Mortal loads of beef and beer.

Famous some were—yet they died:
Poets—Statesmen—Rogues beside,
King—Queens, all of them do rot,
What about them? Now—they're not!

AMANDA McKITTRICK ROS (1860-1939)

Be Merry

WHENEVER you see the hearse go by
And think to yourself that you're gonna die,
Be merry, my friends, be merry.

They put you in a big white shirt
And cover you over with tons of dirt,
Be merry, my friends, be merry.

They put you in a long-shaped box
And cover you over with tons of rocks,
Be merry, my friends, be merry.

The worms crawl out and the worms crawl in,
The ones that crawl in are lean and thin,
The ones that crawl out are fat and stout,
Be merry, my friends, be merry.

Your eyes fall in and your hair falls out
And your brains come tumbling down your snout,
Be merry, my friends, be merry.

ANON

Lines on the Death of Chairman Mao

SO.
Farewell then
Chairman Mao.

You are the
Last of the
Great revolutionary

Figures. You
And I
Had little in
Common

Except that
Like me
You were a poet.

Though how you
Found time
To write poems

In addition to
Running a
Country of
800 million people

Is baffling
Frankly.

E J THRIBB

The Tired Housewife's Epitaph

HERE lies a poor woman who was always tired,
She lived in a house where help wasn't hired.
Her last words on earth were: 'Dear friends, I am going
To where there's no cooking, or washing, or sewing,
For everything there is exact to my wishes,
For where they don't eat there's no washing of dishes.
I'll be where loud anthems will always be ringing,
But having no voice I'll be quit of the singing.
Don't mourn for me now, don't mourn for me never,
I'm going to do nothing for ever and ever.'

ANON

What'll Be the Title?

O TO scuttle from the battle and to settle on an atoll
      far from brutal mortal neath a wattle portal!
To keep little mottled cattle and to whittle down one's
      chattels and not hurtle after brittle yellow metal!
To listen, non-committal, to the anecdotal local tittle-tattle
      on a settle round the kettle,
Never startled by a rattle more than betel-nuts a-prattle or
      the myrtle-petals' subtle throttled chortle!
But I'll bet that what'll happen if you footle round an atoll
      is you'll get in rotten fettle living totally on turtle,
      nettles, cuttle-fish or beetles, victuals fatal to the
      natal *élan-vital*,
And hit the bottle.
I guess I'd settle
For somewhere ethical and practical like Bootle.

JUSTIN RICHARDSON (1900-1975)

Two Ruthless Rhymes

WASTE

I HAD written to Aunt Maud,
Who was on a trip abroad,
When I heard she'd died of cramp
Just too late to save the stamp.

CARELESSNESS

A WINDOW-cleaner in our street
Who fell (five stories) at my feet
Impaled himself on my umbrella.
I said: 'Come, come, you careless fella!
If my umbrella had been shut
You might have landed on my nut.'

HARRY GRAHAM (1874-1936)

The Legatee

IN FAIR San Francisco a good man did dwell,
And he wrote out a will, for he didn't feel well.
Said he: 'It is proper, when making a gift,
To stimulate virtue by comforting thrift.'
So he left all his property, legal and straight,
To 'the cursedest rascal in all of the State.'
But the name he refused to insert, for, said he:
'Let each man consider himself legatee.'
In due course of time that philanthropist died,
And all San Francisco, and Oakland beside—
Save only the lawyers—came each with his claim,
The lawyers preferring to manage the same.
The cases were tried in Department Thirteen,
Judge Murphy presided, sedate and serene,
But couldn't quite specify, legal and straight,
The cursedest rascal in all of the State.
And so he remarked to them, little and big—
To claimants: 'You skip!' and to lawyers: 'You dig!'
They tumbled, tumultuous, out of his court
And left him victorious, holding the fort.
'Twas then that he said: 'It is plain to my mind
This property's ownerless—how can I find
The cursedest rascal in all of the State?'
So he took it himself, which was legal and straight.

AMBROSE BIERCE (1842-1914)

Limerick about Limericks

THERE was a young man of Japan,
Whose limericks never would scan.
When they said it was so,
He replied, 'Yes, I know,
But I always try to get as many words into the
last line as ever I possibly can.'

ANON

FIRST LINE INDEX

ACKNOWLEDGEMENTS

Pam Ayres, 'Oh I Wish I'd Looked After Me Teeth', from 'The Works: Selected Poems' by Pam Ayres, reproduced with the permission of BBC Worldwide Limited. Copyright © Pam Ayres 1992.

Hilaire Belloc, 'Lord Finchley' & 'Lord Heygate', from 'Cautionary Tales'. Reprinted by permission of PFD on behalf of The Estate of Hilaire Belloc © The Estate of Hilaire Belloc.

E C Bentley, 'Clerihews', reproduced with permission of Curtis Brown Group Ltd, London, on behalf of the Estate of E C Bentley. Copyright © E C Bentley.

Sir John Betjeman, 'Hunter Trials' & 'How To Get On In Society', from 'Collected Poems'. Reproduced by the kind permission of John Murray (Publishers) Ltd.

Gary Boswell, 'Ducks Don't Shop At Sainsbury's', reproduced by the kind permission of the author.

Noël Coward, 'The Stately Homes of England', from 'Collected Verse; Noël Coward', edited by Martin Payn & Martin Tickner, published by Methuen Publishing Limited. Copyright © The Estate of Noël Coward.

Roald Dahl, 'St Ives', from 'Rhyme Stew' published by Jonathan Cape & Penguin Books Ltd. Reproduced by the kind permission of David Higham Associates.

'The Hippopotamus Song' - Words by Michael Flanders, Music by Donald Swann © 1952 Chappell Music Ltd, London W6 8BS. Reproduced by permission of International Music Publications Ltd. All Rights Reserved.

Michael Flanders, 'The Walrus', from 'Creatures Great and Small' published by Dobson Books 1964.

John Hegley, 'In the Arms of My Glasses', from 'Can I Come Down Now Dad?' reprinted by permission of PFD on behalf of John Hegley ©: as printed in the original volume.

Miles Kington, 'Mary Mary Quite Contrary', from 'Miles Kington's Motorway Madness'. Reprinted by permission of HarperCollins Publishers Ltd. © Miles Kington 1999.

Richard Mallett, 'Translations from the Ish', reproduced with the permission of Punch, Ltd.

Spike Milligan, 'On the Ning Nang Nong' & 'The Terns', with permission of Spike Milligan Productions Ltd.

Adrian Mitchell, 'Watch Your Step, I'm Drenched', reprinted by permission of PFD on behalf of Adrian Mitchell. Educational Health Warning! Adrian Mitchell asks that none of his poems are used in connection with any examinations whatsoever!

Ogden Nash, 'No Doctors Today, Thank You', 'Peekaboo, I Almost See You' & 'The Octopus', from 'Candy Is Dandy: The Best of Ogden Nash', edited by Ogden Nash, Linell Smith & Isabel Eberstadt, published by Carlton Books 1994. Reprinted with the kind permission of Andre Deutsch Ltd.

Dorothy Parker, 'One Perfect Rose', reprinted by permission of Gerald Duckworth & Co. Ltd.

Justin Richardson, 'What'll Be the Title?', reproduced with the permission of Punch, Ltd.

R E C Stringer, 'Sartorial Solecism', reproduced with the permission of Punch, Ltd.

E J Thribb, 'Lines on the Death of Chairman Mao', copyright Pressdram Limited 200[2]. Reproduced by permission.

Kit Wright, 'Sergeant Brown's Parrot', from 'Rabbiting On', reproduced by the kind permission of the author.